Y0-CAY-837

KAMALA HARRIS

KRISTEN SUSIENKA

PowerKiDS press.

New York

Published in 2020 by The Rosen Publishing Group, Inc.
29 East 21st Street, New York, NY 10010

First Edition

Editor: Kristen Susienka
Book Design: Michael Flynn

Photo Credits: Cover, p. 1 Al Drago/Getty Images; series background Kharchenko Rusian/Shutterstock.com; p. 5 Ethan Miller/Getty Images; p. 7 (paper texture) Color Symphony/Shutterstock.com; p. 7 (map) pingebat/ Shutterstock.com; p. 7 (city skyline) Sundry Photography/Shutterstock.com; p. 9 Jason Binn/WireImage/Getty Images; p. 11 PhotoQuest/Archive Photos/Getty Images; p. 13 Tom Williams/CQ-Roll Call Group/Getty Images; p. 15 MediaNews Group/The Mercury News/Getty Images; p. 17 Bloomberg/Getty Images; p. 19 Barbara Davidson/Los Angeles Times/Getty Images; p. 21 NOAH BERGER/AFP/Getty Images.

Library of Congress Cataloging-in-Publication Data

Names: Susienka, Kristen, author.
Title: Kamala Harris / Kristen Susienka.
Description: New York : PowerKids Press, [2020] | Series: African American
   leaders of courage | Includes index.
Identifiers: LCCN 2019015261| ISBN 9781725311060 (pbk.) | ISBN 9781725311084
   (library bound) | ISBN 9781725311077 (6 pack)
Subjects: LCSH: Harris, Kamala, 1964–Juvenile literature. | United States.
   Congress. Senate–Biography–Juvenile literature. | African American women
   legislators–Biography–Juvenile literature. | Women legislators–United
   States–Biography–Juvenile literature. | Legislators–United
   States–Biography–Juvenile literature. | African American
   politicians–Biography–Juvenile literature. | Women
   politicians–Biography–Juvenile literature.
Classification: LCC E901.1.H37 S87 2020 | DDC 328.73/092 [B] –dc23
LC record available at https://lccn.loc.gov/2019015261

Manufactured in the United States of America
CPSIA Compliance Information: Batch #CWPK20. For Further Information contact Rosen Publishing, New York, New York at 1-800-237-9932.

CONTENTS

A Successful Woman

Kamala (COMMA-lah) Harris is a successful woman helping change **politics** today. For many years, she has worked hard to help others. She believes in **justice**, truth, and equal rights for all. She is a strong woman and role model.

Starting Life

Kamala's father is from Jamaica, and her mother was from India. They met in college in California. They got married and started working in the United States. Kamala was born in Oakland, California, in 1964.

UNITED STATES OF AMERICA

Oakland, California

Family Values

Kamala's parents split up when she was a little girl. She and her sister, Maya, lived mostly with their mom. They grew up in California. Their mother studied cancer, a type of sickness. She also believed in social justice, or equality for all.

Maya Harris

Civil Rights Children

Kamala and her sister grew up during the civil rights movement. This was a time when many people fought for equal rights for African Americans. Kamala's parents took her to many events. She and Maya went to a school with many different kinds of people.

civil rights rally in 1965, Washington, D.C.

Law School

In the 1980s, Kamala went to college. She liked helping people and standing up for others. She studied political science and other subjects. She then went to law school and became a lawyer, or someone whose job is to help people with the law, in 1989.

13

District Attorney and Attorney General

Kamala became **district attorney** of San Francisco in 2004. She became California's first African American and female **attorney general** in 2010. She started new programs to help people who got in trouble for the first time. Her ideas helped change communities for the better.

Making Change

Kamala worked hard to make California a safer place. She helped pass laws and rules to fight crime and hate. For example, she fought a law that would keep same-sex couples from marrying. In time, the law was overturned.

Becoming a U.S. Senator

In 2014, Kamala married Doug Emhoff, a lawyer. In 2016, she became California's second female African American senator. She fought for rights for **immigrants**, women, and workers. She wrote a book about her life in 2019.

Leading the Way

In January 2019, Kamala decided to run for president of the United States. Many people liked her and thought she'd be a good leader. When running, she spoke often about justice and civil rights. She continues to work hard for people today.

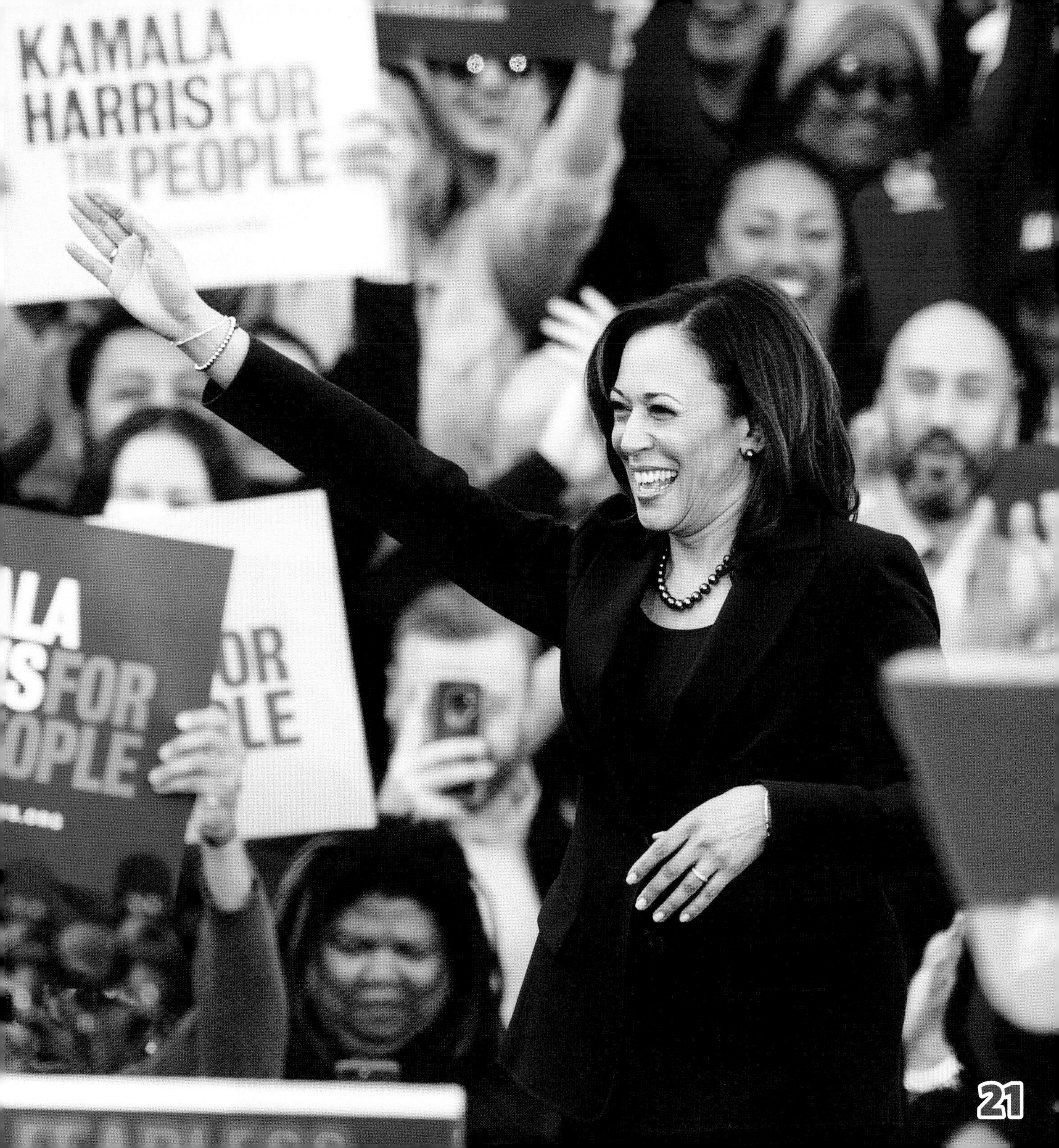
KAMALA
HARRIS FOR
THE PEOPLE

THE LIFE AND CAREER OF KAMALA HARRIS

1964 — Kamala Harris is born.

1989 — Kamala finishes law school.

2010 — Kamala becomes California's first African American and first woman attorney general.

2014 — Kamala marries Doug Emhoff.

2016 — Kamala becomes a U.S. senator for California.

2019 — Kamala announces her presidential campaign.

GLOSSARY

attorney general: The chief lawyer for a country or state.

district attorney: A lawyer who starts law cases against people charged with crimes in a certain state or area.

immigrant: A person who comes to a country to live there.

justice: Fair treatment.

politics: Activities of the government and government officials.

INDEX

WEBSITES

Due to the changing nature of Internet links, PowerKids Press has developed an online list of websites related to the subject of this book. This site is updated regularly. Please use this link to access the list: www.powerkidslinks.com/AALC/harris